CONTENTS

Gary Barlow

Who is Gary Barlow?	4
Gary's Childhood	6
Starting Out	8
Take That	10
Gary Going Solo	12
Take That Reunion	14
The Jubilee Concert	16
Charity Work	18
The X Factor	20
Honours and Awards	22
Family Life	24
Acting and Theatre Projects	26
Are you Best Mates with Gary?	28
Glossary	31
Index	32

Who is GARY BARLOW?

'I QUITE LIKE BEING WHO I AM.'

■ Gary Barlow is an international pop megastar. From performing in working men's clubs to organizing a jubilee concert for the Queen, Gary has come a long way to earn his place as one of Britain's most successful and popular entertainers.

NAME: Gary Barlow

BORN: 20 January 1971

FAMILY: Married to Dawn, with children Daniel, Emily and Daisy

HOMETOWN: Frodsham, Cheshire, England

SCHOOLS: Weaver Vale Primary School and Frodsham High School

OCCUPATION: Singer, songwriter, composer, record producer

FAMOUS FOR: Take That and his solo career

LIKES: Coffee, music, writing songs, playing piano and going to the cinema

Gary's Childhood

Gary Barlow came into this world on 20 January 1971. Right from the start he was a star in the making, always singing and dancing to keep his family entertained.

Gary grew up in the small market town of Frodsham in Cheshire with his big brother, Ian, and their mum and dad, Colin and Marjorie. He went to the local schools, Weaver Vale Primary and Frodsham High School.

As a kid, Gary got 50 pence pocket money a week. It wasn't enough to buy all the albums he wanted, but his life was still filled with the music that his parents played around the house. They loved the Beatles, Motown music and the Bee Gees – all music from the 1960s and 1970s. Gary soon developed a taste of his own for pop songs. He watched *Top of the Pops* every week, forbidding anyone in the room from talking while it was on.

As Gary watched his pop idols perform, his greatest wish was to be up there with them. At the age of nine he longed to sing with Elton John – a dream that was later to come true.

When Gary saw the band Depeche Mode perform their hit single *Just Can't Get Enough*, he was mesmerized. He asked for a keyboard for Christmas and then spent the next few years teaching himself how to play his favourite songs – and writing some of his own. He was inspired by the music of the 1980s, describing it as 'his era'. The 1983 hit *New Song* by Howard Jones was a big favourite for Gary when he was 12.

TAKE THIS!
Gary took packed lunches to school and confesses to eating his chocolate biscuit first and then not eating his sandwiches!

'I WAS ONE OF THOSE KIDS THAT'S FOREVER DANCING IN FRONT OF THE TV LOOKING AT MY REFLECTION.'

At the age of 15, Gary entered a television competition on the BBC daytime show *Pebble Mill at One* to write a Christmas song. His effort *Let's Pray for Christmas* earned him a place in the finals and he was invited to record his entry at a studio in London.

Starting Out

At the age of 16 Gary left school and began to perform in working men's clubs around the north of England.

He spent several evenings a week performing, helped by his parents who drove him and all his equipment to the clubs and pubs where he was singing. The money he earned was spent on musical equipment which soon filled up his bedroom.

Gary's days were spent song-writing and recording in his over-crowded bedroom. The demo tapes he made were sent to one record label after another but received little interest. One record company executive even threw his demo tape out of the window. Gary didn't let the rejection put him off his quest for stardom; his ambition never faded and he didn't give up his dream.

'IT HAD REACHED THE STAGE WHERE THERE WAS NO ROOM IN MY BEDROOM FOR A BED, SO FOR THREE YEARS I SLEPT ON THE COUCH IN THE LOUNGE.'

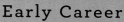

In 1989, Gary appointed an agent, Barry Woolley, and recorded a single, Love is in the Air, which was never released. He also had some professional photos of himself taken by celebrity photographer, Michael Braham. Michael was a good friend of casting agent Nigel Martin-Smith and introduced Gary to him. Inspired by the success of a group called New Kids on the Block, Nigel was in the process of setting up a boy band. After hearing some of Gary's recordings, he decided that the young performer would make the perfect lead-singer. The name of the band was Take That!

TAKE THIS!

Gary's early composition A Million Love Songs was one of the songs that impressed Nigel Martin-Smith when they first met. It featured on the first Take That album.

TAKE THAT

Nigel Martin-Smith built his boy band around Gary's song-writing talent, but there was still some way to go before Take That became a success.

Take That spent two years playing live at pubs, clubs and even in school assembly halls. Slowly, they were building a fan base, but their first three singles only just made it into the music charts.

Gary was joined by:

Mark Owen,
who had been working in a bank

Howard Donald,
who had been spraying cars

Jason Orange,
who was a a professional dancer

Robbie Williams,
who had been at school studying for exams

1992

In 1992 they released an album, Take That and Party. The next three singles they released from this became hits. The first, It Only Takes a Minute, reached number seven. The next two singles, I Found Heaven and A Million Love Songs, also reached the top ten. Finally they had made it big!

1993

Hot on the heels of their success, Take That released their second album, *Everything Changes*, in 1993. This album also used Gary's original material and reached number one in the album charts. They released six singles from it – all hits. The band now had fans across Europe and Asia, although they still hadn't broken into the American market.

TAKE THIS!

The single Back for Good sold nearly 350,000 copies in its first week. It stayed at number one for four weeks, by which time it had sold nearly 1 million copies.

1995

When Take That released their third album, *Nobody Else*, in 1995 their success continued. Their most successful single from this album, and from their career to date, was *Back for Good*, which reached the number one spot in 31 countries across the globe. This was also their first American hit, with the song reaching number seven on the US *Billboard* charts.

Take That went on a world tour in 1995 without Robbie Williams, who had left the band shortly before.

1996

Although the band remained as popular as ever with just the four of them, Take That made the decision to split up in 1996.

GARY GOING SOLO

Gary wasted no time in launching his solo career, which was predicted to be a huge success by the media and his fans.

His first two solo singles, *Forever Love* and *Love Won't Wait*, were both number one hits in the UK charts. His album, *Open Road*, was also a chart-topper, selling two million copies worldwide.

Twelve Months, Eleven Days was the title of Gary's second solo album, which he released in 1999. This and the first two singles released from it did not do so well. Gary parted company with his record label and for the next five years he stayed away from the public eye.

Gary has talked about this time in his life, explaining that he felt very depressed:

'IT WASN'T NOT BEING FAMOUS ANY MORE, OR EVEN NOT BEING A RECORDING ARTIST. IT WAS HAVING NOBODY WHO NEEDED ME, NO PHONES RINGING, NOTHING TO DO.'

'IT WAS ALL A BIT OF A TORMENT. I HAD THIS BEAUTIFUL WHITE PIANO, MY LUCKY PIANO. EVERY HIT I HAD WAS WRITTEN ON THIS PIANO. WITHIN S MONTHS OF THIS NOT HAPPENING ANY MOR THIS PIANO DROVE ME MAD.'

With his solo career on hold, Gary signed a publishing deal with music comapny Sony and continued to write songs. After spending six months in America on a song-writing project, he returned to the UK and wrote and produced songs for performers including Charlotte Church and Shirley Bassey.

2005

Gary returned to the public eye when Take That reformed in 2005 (see page 14).

2011

In 2011, Gary turned 40 and decided to celebrate his birthday in style; he announced that he would perform a concert at the Shepherd's Bush Empire. The experience clearly agreed with him and he went on to perform two full solo concerts, the first in 11 years, at the Royal Albert Hall. The money raised from these concerts went to charity (see page 18).

2012

In 2012, Gary announced that he would be touring the UK and Ireland, saying:

'I'M REALLY EXCITED ABOUT THESE DATES. PLAYING LIVE IS MY FAVOURITE THING AND I HAVEN'T PLAYED A SOLO SHOW FOR OVER A YEAR NOW. LAST YEAR PLAYING TWO LONDON SHOWS WAS BRILLIANT. WE ALL HAD SUCH A GOOD TIME, SO I THOUGHT RIGHT LET'S GET OUT AND SEE THE REST OF THE COUNTRY!'

TAKE THAT REUNION

When ITV made a documentary called _Take That: For the Record_, it was the beginning of a new era for Gary.

The documentary aired in 2005 and featured the band members talking about their fame and the success that Take That had enjoyed during the 1990s. The programme was so popular with the viewers that the band decided to get back together, still without Robbie Williams, and go on tour.

The tour was a sell-out and their first single release after their reunion, _Patience_, went to number one in the UK charts. It stayed there for four weeks and topped the charts across Europe. Their next single, _Shine_, was also a number one hit, as was their album, _Beautiful World_, which was released at the end of 2006.

TAKE THIS!

Although on a break, Take That did get together to play at the closing ceremony of the 2012 Olympics in London.

By the end of 2008, Take That were still going strong and released another hit album, *The Circus*. That year they won two Brit Awards – one for Best British Single and one for Best British Live Act. Their 2009 UK tour, Take That Presents: The Circus Live, sold over one million tickets in a matter of hours and was a massive success.

Gary was busy writing new material to satisfy the voracious hunger of the Take That fans for his songs. The next album, released in 2010, was *Progress*. This was the first work to include Robbie Williams since 1995. Gary remarked: 'It's like therapy, that record, what it did for us all and where it took us as friends.'

At the end of 2011, Take That announced that they would be taking a break to give them time to work on projects outside the band.

'WE HAVE A WIDER AUDIENCE BECAUSE THE RECORDS HAVE BEEN GOOD, BUT I THINK OUR CORE FAN WAS PROBABLY A FAN THE FIRST TIME ROUND, WHICH IS SO LOVELY.'

'WHEN WE'RE TOGETHER AND WORKING AS A BAND EVERYONE HAS THEIR SPACE, SEVEN O'CLOCK COMES AND EVERYONE GOES HOME. IT'S NOT AS FULL-ON AS IT WAS THE FIRST TIME, WHERE WE SPENT EVERY MINUTE OF THE DAY TOGETHER.'

The Jubilee Concert

In 2012, the Queen celebrated her Diamond Jubilee, marking 60 years on the throne. Gary played a big part in the celebrations by organising a concert at Buckingham Palace and co-writing the official Diamond Jubilee song.

When Gary and Andrew Lloyd Webber were approached to write a song for the Queen's Diamond Jubilee, they began by asking Prince Charles about the kind of music that his mother would like to hear. He told them that the Queen was particularly proud of the Commonwealth, and so it was decided that the song would use influences from all of the Commonwealth countries. Gary set off first for Kenya, the country where the Queen had been when she heard the sad news of her father's death and that she had ascended to the throne.

Take This!

Prince Harry met up with Gary in Jamaica and was recorded playing the tambourine. This track was included in his grandmother's special song.

Once Gary had written the words to the song, he began to meet with singers and musicians to record tracks for the single. The African Children's Choir provided vocals, while a Kenyan percussion group, The Slum Drummers, were recorded using instruments made from items of rubbish.

During his visit to Jamaica, Gary recorded a young Rastafarian boy who played drums. In Australia, Gary found use for the talents of a blind Aboriginal singer and acoustic guitarist before heading off to the Sydney Opera House to record a full symphony orchestra. Back in England, the Military Wives Choir added the finishing touches and the song was complete.

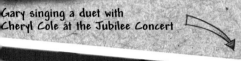
Gary singing a duet with Cheryl Cole at the Jubilee Concert

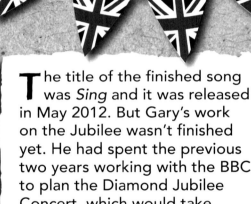

The title of the finished song was *Sing* and it was released in May 2012. But Gary's work on the Jubilee wasn't finished yet. He had spent the previous two years working with the BBC to plan the Diamond Jubilee Concert, which would take place in June 2012 outside Buckingham Palace on The Mall. The concert included performances from many famous artists including Robbie Williams, Kylie Minogue, Sir Tom Jones, Dame Shirley Bassey, will.i.am, Annie Lennox and Gary himself, performing with Cheryl Cole.

The Diamond Jubilee song, *Sing*, was performed at the concert for the first time in front of the Queen and other members of the Royal Family.

Charity Work

Throughout his career, Gary has demonstrated his social conscience. Through the many charities he has worked with, he has raised millions of pounds to help disadvantaged people all over the world.

In March 2009, Gary arranged a climb to the top of Mount Kilimanjaro, the highest mountain in Africa, to raise money for Comic Relief. He was in good company: his climbing buddies included Cheryl Cole, Ronan Keating, Alesha Dixon and Chris Moyles.

Gary took part in Simon Cowell's Helping Haiti project after a devastating earthquake struck the Caribbean country in 2010. The single, *Everybody Hurts*, was a massive hit, raising much-needed funds for the appeal. Later that year, Gary performed the song *Shame* with Robbie Williams at Twickenham Stadium to raise money for Help for Heroes – a charity supporting war veterans.

In 2011, Gary donated all proceeds from his 40th birthday performance at the Shepherd's Bush Empire and two concerts at the Royal Albert Hall to the Prince's Trust, a charity headed by Prince Charles. Also that year, Gary organized a gala concert for the annual BBC charity appeal Children in Need.

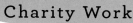

Blackpool
Tower

When the northern seaside town of Blackpool was in trouble in 2013, Gary went to the rescue. He stepped in to turn on the famous Blackpool Illuminations when the act originally booked had to pull out. On condition that the organizers made a contribution to Children in Need, Gary switched on the lights and played a selection of his hit songs to a crowd of 5,000 people.

In 2013, Gary left *The X-Factor* live results show in a bit of a hurry; he was on his way to meet troops in Afghanistan. There he spent time talking to soldiers and played a concert for them to boost their moral and thank them for their hard work.

'I HOPE THE MONEY RAISED THROUGH THESE CONCERTS (AT SHEPHERD'S BUSH AND THE ROYAL ALBERT HALL) WILL MAKE A REAL DIFFERENCE TO YOUNG LIVES. IT'S REALLY IMPORTANT TO ME THAT DISADVANTAGED YOUNG PEOPLE GET THE SUPPORT THEY NEED.'

The X-FACTOR

Simon Cowell was a hard act to follow when he left the hit ITV talent show *The X Factor*, but Gary stepped in and made his mark on the show.

Gary joined *The X Factor* as a judge in 2011 to work alongside Louis Walsh, Tulisa Contostavlos and Kelly Rowland. He was given the Boys' category and mentored Marcus Collins who was a runner up in the final that year. Gary took his role seriously and continued to work with Marcus after the show ended. He helped him to release his debut album which made it to the top ten of the charts.

'WHEN YOU'RE IN A BAND... YOU'RE IN THIS BUBBLE, AND NO ONE'S ALLOWED TOO CLOSE, BUT WITH THIS SHOW THE LID IS LIFTED ON EVERYTHING, AND IT'S JUST YOU.'

In 2012, Gary returned to the series, with Nicole Sherzinger replacing Kelly Rowland as a judge. For this series, Gary was given the 'Overs' category which meant he was working with both male and female artists over the age of 28. Gary saw Christopher Maloney, a former call centre operative from Liverpool, through to the finals where he was runner-up to that year's winner, James Arthur.

Joining the show for a third time in 2013, Gary worked with Sharon Osbourne who had returned to replace Tulisa as a judge. It wasn't to be third time lucky for Gary; he was in charge of the 'Groups' category this time and worked with Rough Copy, who made it through to the semi-final – the eventual winner was Sam Bailey.

'I'VE HAD AN AMAZING TIME ON X FACTOR THESE PAST THREE YEARS. A SHOW LIKE THIS NEEDS TO STAY FRESH AND EXCITING SO IT'S A GREAT OPPORTUNITY FOR SOMEONE TO COME IN AND TAKE THE SHOW PAST ITS INCREDIBLE TEN YEAR ANNIVERSARY.'

Gary announced that he would not be returning to *The X Factor* line-up in 2014.

21

Honours and Awards

Gary has been working in the music industry for many years and his hard work and talent have been recognized by many.

In June 2012, Gary learned he would receive an OBE (Order of the British Empire) from the Queen for his services to the entertainment industry and to charity. He went to collect his medal in November that year, having already framed a certificate from the Queen that had previously been sent to him.

'I ENJOY EVERY MINUTE OF THE WORK I DO, WITH A LOT OF IT BEING A REWARD IN ITSELF, SO FOR SOMEBODY TO DECIDE I SHOULD GET RECOGNIZED FOR THAT IS JUST AMAZING. MY FAMILY ARE VERY PROUD.'

'I'M ABSOLUTELY THRILLED AND FEEL VERY PRIVILEGED TO BE IN THE COMPANY OF SO MANY BRILLIANT PEOPLE WHO I KNOW HAVE RECEIVED AN OBE... GROWING UP I NEVER DREAMT THAT ONE DAY I'D BE GETTING ONE MYSELF.'

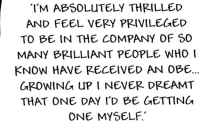

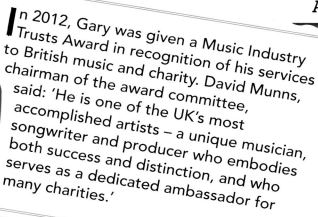

In 2012, Gary was given a Music Industry Trusts Award in recognition of his services to British music and charity. David Munns, chairman of the award committee, said: 'He is one of the UK's most accomplished artists – a unique musician, songwriter and producer who embodies both success and distinction, and who serves as a dedicated ambassador for many charities.'

Take This!
Possibly Gary's most prestigious prize to date is his Gold Blue Peter badge, awarded to him in 2009 for 'outstanding achievements and inspiring children to realize their talents and achieve'.

Gary won a Q magazine Award in 2011 for 'classic songwriter'. And, in 2012, GQ magazine gave him its 'outstanding achievement' award.

In addition to the numerous music awards won by Take That, Gary has received six Ivor Novello awards. This award is named after the famous Welsh composer (1914–1951) and is given out to the most successful composers and songwriters. Gary received awards for writing five songs: Pray, Back for Good, Never Forget, Shine and The Flood. The sixth award was for Songwriter of the Year in 1993. Although it was Take That who performed the hit songs, it was Gary who had written them, so the awards went to him.

FAMILY LIFE

Gary met his wife, Dawn Andrews, in 1995 when she joined the Nobody Else tour with Take That as a dancer. Gary and Dawn married in 2000. They live with their three children – Daniel, Emily and Daisy.

Gary describes his own childhood as 'a faultless upbringing of complete stability' and says that to leave home feeling like you believe in relationships and you believe in life, as he did, is something he tries to bring to his own family.

Gary in Los Angeles, USA, with his wife Dawn and children Daniel, Emily and Daisy

'AS A PARENT NOW, THAT'S ALL I WANT TO DO FOR MY CHILDREN, TO SHOW THEM WHAT A HAPPY HOME IS, AND SUPPORT THEM WITH WHATEVER THEY WANT TO DO.'

Gary's family have to live in the public eye. His children know what he does for a living and so do the other children they go to school with. 'Dan's in a class where all his mates know who I am. He and Emily know what I do, but they're not those kids who think they've got everything, they're really not. This far I'm so proud of how we've brought them up.' Gary has said that keeping a balance between his work life and his family life is good for him. When he has been up late at awards parties he finds himself thinking things like: 'I'm going to be woken up in five hours, they're all going to jump in my bed.'

Gary describes himself as having the opposite personality to his wife, Dawn. He says that's probably what makes their relationship so strong. 'All the stuff I do is her worst nightmare… walking into a room and having everyone look at you, that's her absolute worst nightmare on earth. Whereas I love it.'

Take This!

Gary loves to cook and keep the house tidy! He is the cook of the family and claims to make great soups!

Acting and Theatre Projects

Not just a great singer and talented songwriter, Gary has another string to his bow – acting!

Gary got his first acting role in the ITV1 drama *Heartbeat*, a period police drama. He played the part of hitch-hiker Micky Shannon. Since the episode aired in 2000, Gary has joked that he drew on the experience while acting in his video for the song *Let Me Go*. 'I had to draw on my experience from *Heartbeat*… I don't know why it was called *Heartbeat* because, believe me, in my performance there wasn't a heartbeat, it was more like flat-line.'

Gary Barlow filming for
Keith Lemon: The Film
in London, UK

Although he clearly wasn't pleased with his first performance, Gary gave acting another go 12 years later when he appeared in the movie *Keith Lemon: The Film*. This British comedy film starred Leigh Francis who plays Keith Lemon. There were other cameo appearances in the film from stars including Ronan Keating, Peter Andre, Jedward, Emma Bunton and Fearne Cotton.

Gary surprised everyone by kissing Miranda in her hit show of the same name in 2013. When asked how the cameo role came about, he explained: 'She emailed me, I think, and said, "Here's a crazy idea" – and I said absolutely no way on earth! And then I got an email about three months later saying, "We're really desperate now, we haven't got anything going on in this episode – will you be in it?"... So I thought well yeah, let's do it!' Gary went on to say that they had not rehearsed the scene, but completed it in two takes. We did it twice – just because I wanted to kiss her again! It was so minty!' One show insider said: 'Gary was charming on set and a natural when it came to delivering his lines.'

Take This!

Gary has also turned his hand to musical theatre. He has worked on a new musical version of Finding Neverland. The musical is about the personal life of J.M. Barrie, the author of Peter Pan. 'This is something I've always wanted to do, so it's a real privilege to be involved,' said Gary. Harvey Weinstein, the show's producer, described Gary as 'one of the finest songwriters in the world'.

ARE YOU BEST MATES WITH...

Gary Barlow

By now you should know lots of things about Gary. Test your knowledge of him by answering these questions:

1 Which TV show made Gary dance when he was a kid?

a) Top of the Pops
b) Doctor Who
c) Blue Peter

2 Where did Gary live as a boy?

a) Brighton
b) Frodsham
c) Brooklyn

3 At what age did Gary leave school?

a) 18
b) 16
c) 14

4 Which TV comedian did Gary kiss?

a) Miranda
b) Jo Brand
c) Harry Hill

5 Why couldn't Gary sleep in his bedroom?

a) Because he was too tired to climb the stairs
b) Because he was scared of the dark
c) Because it was filled with musical equipment

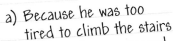

6 What was Gary's first toy?

a) A recorder
b) A keyboard
c) A drum kit

7 What is Gary's wife called?
   a) Melody
   b) Belinda
   c) Dawn

8 What was Take That's first top ten hit?
   a) It Only Takes a Minute
   b) It Takes a Long Time
   c) Where Did the Time Go?

9 Which popular television drama did Gary appear on?
   a) Holby City
   b) Eastenders
   c) Heartbeat

10 Which award did Gary win six times?
   a) Ivor Novello
   b) Grammy
   c) BAFTA

Answers

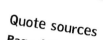

1   a) *Top of the Pops*
2   b) Frodsham
3   b) 16
4   a) Miranda
5   c) It was filled with
        musical equipment
6   b) A keyboard
7   c) Dawn
8   a) *It Only Takes a Minute*
9   c) *Heartbeat*
10   a) Ivor Novello

Quote sources

Page 4 The Guardian, 2011; Page 7 BBC News, 2012; Page 8 The Telegraph, 2012; Page 12 The Telegraph, 2012; Page 13 Press release statement, 2012; Page 15 The Telegraph, 2012; Page 19 theroyalalberthall.com, 2011; Page 20 The Telegraph, 2012; Page 21 The Huffington Post, 2013; Page 22 BBC News, 2012; Page 25 The Telegraph, 2012; Page 27 The Graham Norton Show, 2013

You can find out more about Gary Barlow by:
logging onto
http://www.garybarlow.com
or following him on
Twitter @GaryBarlow

You can read more about Gary in the following books:

My Take by Gary Barlow and Richard Havers (Bloomsbury, 2006)
Gary: The Definitive Biography of Gary Barlow by Sean Smith (Simon and Schuster, 2013)
Gary Barlow: Time to Shine – The Unauthorised Biography by Justin Lewis (John Blake Publishing, 2013)

Glossary

Aboriginal
People whose ancestors originated from the Australian continent

Ambassador
An official representative

Annie Lennox
A famous singer most popular in the 1980s

Beatles (The)
The most famous band of the 1960s, still popular to this day around the world

Bee Gees (The)
A band famous from the 1960s and 1970s made up of the Gibbs brothers

Buckingham Palace
An official residence of the Queen

Debut
A first performance in public

Depeche Mode
An electronic pop band most popular in the 1980s

Diamond Jubilee
The celebration of the 60th anniversary of the Queen's reign

Era
A particular period of time

Howard Jones
A famous 1980s pop star

Morale
A person's confidence and enthusiasm

Motown music
Music originating from the American city of Detroit, also known as motor town, or motown for short

Rastafarian
A person belonging to the Rastafari movement – holding a set of spiritual ideas that became popular in Jamaica

Shirley Bassey
A Welsh singer and one of the 20th century's most popular performers

The Mall
The road leading up to Buckingham Palace

Top of the Pops
A BBC music show broadcast between 1964 and 2006

Voracious
To have a huge appetite for something

Working men's clubs
Social clubs for working men in communities around Britain

INDEX

A

acting 26–27
African Children's Choir
    17
Andrews, Dawn 24, 25

B

Bassey, Shirley 13, 17
birth 5, 6
Blackpool Illuminations
    19
boy bands 9, 10–11
Braham, Michael 9
Brit awards 15

C

charity work 13, 18–19,
    22, 23
Charles, Prince of Wales
    16, 18
childhood 6–7, 24
Children in Need 18, 19
Church, Charlotte 13
Cole, Cheryl 17, 18
Collins, Marcus 20
Comic Relief 18
Contostavlos, Tulisa 20,
    21
Cowell, Simon 18, 20

D

demo tapes 8
Depeche Mode 7
depression 12
Diamond Jubilee 16–17
Dixon, Alesha 18
Donald, Howard 10

E

early love of music 6–7
education 5, 6
Elizabeth, Queen 16,
    17, 22

F

family 5, 6, 8, 24–25
Finding Neverland 27
Frodsham 6

G

Gold Blue Peter badge 23

H

Harry, Prince 16
Heartbeat 26
Help for Heroes 18
Helping Haiti 18
honours and awards 22–23

I

Ivor Novello awards 23

J

John, Elton 7
Jones, Howard 7
Jubilee Concert 16–17

K

Keating, Ronan 18, 26
Keith Lemon: The Film 26

L

likes 5
Lloyd Webber, Andrew 16
London Olympics 2012 14

M

marriage and children 5,
    24–25
Martin-Smith, Nigel 9, 10
Military Wives Choir 17
Miranda 27
Moyles, Chris 18
musical theatre 27

O

OBE 22
Orange, Jason 10
Osbourne, Sharon 21
Owen, Mark 10

P

Pebble Mill 7
Prince's Trust 18

Q

quiz 28–29

R

Rowland, Kelly 20

S

Sherzinger, Nicole 20
singles and albums 9,
    10–11, 12, 14, 15
Slum Drummers 17
solo career 12–13
song-writing 7, 8, 9, 11,
    12, 13, 15, 16, 17, 18,
    23, 27

T

Take That 9, 10–11, 13,
    14–15, 23, 24
The X-Factor 19, 20–21
Top of the Pops 6

W

Walsh, Louis 20
Weinstein, Harvey 27
Williams, Robbie 10, 11,
    14, 15, 17, 18
Woolley, Barry 9
working men's clubs 8

Gary Barlow

Singer, Songwriter, Producer

Published in paperback in 2016 by Wayland
Copyright © Wayland 2016

Wayland, an imprint of
Hachette Children's Group
Part of Hodder & Stoughton
Carmelite House
50 Victoria Embankment
London EC4Y 0DZ

MIX
Paper from
responsible sources
FSC® C104740

Senior editor: Julia Adams

Produced for Wayland by Dynamo
Written by Hettie Bingham

Picture acknowledgements:
Key: b=bottom, t=top, r=right, l=left, m=middle, bgd=background

Corbis p7 bl, p22 bl Pool/Reuters; p16 br, 29 br David Moir/Reuters.
Getty Images p2 tr, p4 m, p5 tr, p5 bm, p8, p10 bl, p11 bl, p12 bl,
p15 b, p19 br, p21 m, p25 tr, p30 tr Getty Images. **Rex Features** P1 m,
13 bl Rex Features. **Shutterstock** Backgrounds and Doodles: tsaplia,
casejustin, daisybee, Curly Pat, Veronika Taurus. P6 ml Virinaflora, bl
Asaf Eliason, bl donatas1205, p7 m Cidonia, p9 br PhotoGraphyca, br
PhotoHouse, p19 tl Pefkos, p23 tl Alex_Po. **Splash News** 18 bl Allpix/
Splash News, 20 ml Mercury Press/Splash News, 14 mr, 26 m Splash
News.

Dewey classification: 782.4'2164'092-dc23

ISBN 978 0 7502 8955 9
Library e-book ISBN 987 0 7502 8779 1

Printed in China
10 9 8 7 6 5 4 3 2 1

An Hachette UK company
www.hachette.co.uk
www.hachettechildrens.co.uk

The website addresses (URLs) included in this book were valid at the
time of going to press. However, because of the nature of the internet,
it is possible that some addresses may have changed or some sites may
have closed down since publication. While the author and Publisher
regret any inconvenience this may cause, no responsibility for any such
changes can be accepted by either the author or the Publisher.